October 2011

John + Robin,
    Come and visit
the EAST Coast with us!

            Tory + Anne
            Rockecharlie

Our
Virginia

Pat and Chuck Blackley

Voyageur Press

First published in 2006 by Voyageur Press, an imprint of MBI Publishing Company, Galtier Plaza, Suite 200, 380 Jackson Street, St. Paul, MN 55101-3885 USA

MBI Publishing Company titles are also available at discounts in bulk quantity for industrial or sales-promotional use. For details write to Special Sales Manager at MBI Publishing Company, Galtier Plaza, Suite 200, 380 Jackson Street, St. Paul, MN 55101-3885 USA

Library of Congress Cataloging-in-Publication Data

Blackley, Pat.
  Our Virginia / Pat and Chuck Blackley
    p. cm.
  ISBN-13: 978-0-7603-2639-8
  ISBN-10: 0-7603-2639-8
  1. Virginia—Pictorial works. 2. Virginia—Description and travel. 3. Virginia—History, Local—Pictorial works. I. Blackley, Chuck. II. Title.
    F227.B57 2006
    917.55—dc22

Editor: Josh Leventhal
Designer: Mandy Iverson

Printed in China

On the front cover: George Washington's Mount Vernon Estate and Gardens, viewed from the east lawn at sunrise.

Page 1: Period fireworks light up the Governor's Palace at Colonial Williamsburg during the annual Grand Illumination festival, which marks the beginning of Williamsburg's busy holiday season.

Page 2: A stunning sunrise ushers in a new day at a Virginia Beach fishing pier. Quiet and serene at this early hour, the popular beach will soon be crowded with thousands of eager sun worshippers and wave riders.

Page 3: Built by Ed Mabry around 1910, the Mabry Mill, on the Blue Ridge Parkway, is still grinding grain.

Page 4: From the Pinnacle Overlook in Cumberland Gap National Historical Park, the view looks into the "gap" in the Appalachian Mountains and to Tennessee and Kentucky beyond.

Page 5: On a farm in Madison County, brilliant orange foliage and a predominantly placed pumpkin announce the arrival of fall.

Title page: Viewed from a Browntown overlook in Shenandoah National Park, the sun drops below a cloud and lights the rolling hills of the Shenandoah Valley below.

Title page, inset: Gloucester's charming Courthouse Square looks especially pretty in April during the Daffodil Festival, a celebration of the historical daffodil industry of the Middle Peninsula.

Facing page: In April, acres of bluebells and other spring wildflowers burst into bloom at the Bull Run Regional Park, near Manassas.

About the Authors

Pat and Chuck Blackley are a photographic and writing team born and raised in Virginia. Although they work throughout North America, their concentration is on the eastern United States. With a love of the outdoors and history, they find a wealth of subjects throughout the mid-Atlantic, with their native Virginia a favorite subject. They have enjoyed traveling together to all corners of the Commonwealth for more than thirty years. Chuck is a member of the American Society of Media Photographers.

The Blackleys' previous books include *Blue Ridge Parkway Impressions, Shenandoah National Park Impressions, Shenandoah Valley Impressions,* and *Outer Banks Impressions.* In addition, their work has appeared in numerous magazines, including *Backpacker, Blue Ridge Country, Country, Country Discoveries, Destinations, Endless Vacation, Frommer's Budget Travel, Luxury Living, On Earth, Outdoor America,* and *Outdoor Photographer,* and in books published by Capstone Press, Cherbo Publishing Group, Countryman Press, Farcountry Press, Frommer's, Globe Pequot, Insight Guides, National Geographic, Publications International, Reader's Digest, Sierra Press, and Ulysses Press, among others. Additionally, their photographs appear regularly in calendars, commercial projects, and other publications by organizations such as Boundless Journeys, Comda, Friends of the Blue Ridge Parkway, KC Publications, National Park Service, Pace Communications, Red House Records, Sierra Club, Sony Records, Tide-mark Press, Valley Conservation Council, Wilderness Society, and Willow Creek Press.

Contents

Acknowledgments

We are grateful to all the wonderful people we encountered in our travels throughout Virginia who helped us in so many ways as we worked on this book. Some became willing models in our photographs, while others passed along helpful hints and information about attractions, events, and picturesque places. To all of them, we give our heartfelt thanks. They reminded us constantly of how truly friendly, witty, warm, and hospitable the people of Virginia really are.

We also want to thank and acknowledge the assistance of the following organizations and businesses that helped us to capture the images in this book and provided us with valuable information. In many cases, individuals with these organizations came in at off hours to accommodate our shooting schedule and spent hours with us while we photographed. We truly appreciate their efforts on our behalf: Mount Vernon Ladies' Association, which owns and operates George Washington's Mount Vernon Estate and Gardens; Jamestown-Yorktown Foundation; Colonial Williamsburg Foundation; Thomas Jefferson Foundation, Inc., owner and operator of Monticello; Washington & Lee University, which owns and operates the Lee Chapel and Museum; Arlington National Cemetery; Northrop Grumman Newport News; Chincoteague Chamber of Commerce; Chincoteague Volunteer Fire Department; the Virginia State Senate and the Virginia House of Delegates and their clerks' offices; Appomattox Court House National Historical Park; Henricus Historical Park; Jefferson Hotel; Billy Bain and the Virginia Peanut Growers Association; Blandford Church; Luray Caverns; Natural Bridge of Virginia; Marriott Ranch; Elks National Home; Orange County Hunt Club; Middleburg Spring Races; Foxfield Races; Old Fiddler's Convention; and Urbanna Oyster Festival.

In addition, our thanks also go to the organizations and individuals who kindly provided their assistance, but did not make it into the book.

Finally, we thank our editor at Voyageur Press, Josh Leventhal, for his guidance on this project and for patiently addressing our multitude of questions.

Opposite page: Ash-Lawn Highland, the home of America's fifth president, James Monroe, is located just up the road from Monticello, the home of his good friend Thomas Jefferson. President Monroe makes an appearance during a Plantation Days Festival at Ash-Lawn Highland.

Introduction

Virginia: The Birthplace of America

On the morning of May 13, 1607, three small ships glided silently through the placid waters of the James River in a place called Virginia, part of the "New World."

The vessels had set sail from their homeport of London, England, nearly five months earlier, carrying 104 intrepid, would-be colonists, each one intent on reaping the untold riches of this promising, but still largely unknown, new land.

They anchored the fleet along a low and marshy peninsula that protruded from the north bank of the James, at a site the expedition's leaders found suitable for their settlement. Calling their new home Jamestown—after their sovereign, King James—the eager, albeit sorely naïve and unprepared, group of colonists set about building the first permanent English town in what would ultimately become the most powerful nation in the world. And, the rest, as they say, is history.

Ah yes, history. It's the word that, above all others, defines Virginia. For, as would be expected when discussing the birthplace of a nation, you cannot speak of Virginia without speaking of its history. And no matter where in the Old Dominion you go, it's there, just begging to be told. This commonwealth wears its history proudly and boasts about it at every opportunity, like an old soldier recounting war stories as he shows off his medals and battle scars.

History lurks behind the doors of centuries-old plantation houses in Tidewater and tiny log cabins in the Blue Ridge Mountains. It's found in the timeworn pew boxes of colonial-era churches where George Washington and other patriots once worshiped. It's emblazoned on monuments, recited in plays and musicals, celebrated in festivals, and painted on murals. It's felt in the rhythmic drumbeats of an Indian powwow, as Native Americans, whose ancestors watched those first colonists come ashore, tell of their proud heritage through music and dance.

Nowhere else in America is the past as alive and intrinsic as it is in Virginia. When you walk the streets of Colonial Williamsburg, you can feel the ghosts of our nation's forefathers trodding along beside you. Listen, and you can almost hear the heated discussions of founding fathers like Thomas Jefferson and Patrick Henry as they debate the issues that led to the American Revolution.

You can wander through Virginia's battlefields on trails that cross green meadows and gentle, rolling hillsides. These hallowed grounds lie peaceful and serene now, in such stark contrast to the horrors that once beset them. The Old Dominion has seen more than its share of bloodshed over the last four hundred years. During the Civil War, more battles were fought here and more casualties suffered than in any other state. And, the battles and ultimate surrenders that ended both the Revolutionary and Civil wars took place here, in Yorktown and Appomattox, respectively.

On a lighter note, Virginia's lists of "most" and "first" are long and impressive.

That brilliant flash of scarlet you see flitting from tree to tree is most likely a cardinal, Virginia's state bird.

Opposite page: *Sunset's warm glow paints the bow of the re-created* Susan Constant, *largest of the three ships that carried the first English settlers to America in 1607. She, along with the* Discovery *and* Godspeed, *are moored along the banks of the James River at Jamestown Settlement.*

Spring floral displays enhance the beauty of Thomas Jefferson's Monticello. Jefferson designed two elements into the gardens at Monticello: a winding walkway covering the perimeter of the West Lawn, accompanied by a narrow border of flowers and twenty oval beds immediately around the house.

The arrival of spring in Virginia is heralded by the prolific blossoms of the dogwood, which serves as both the state flower and the state tree.

American presidents, for instance, earns the top spot on both lists. The state has produced a total of eight, making it the undisputed "mother of presidents." In fact, seven of the first twelve presidents were Virginians, including the likes of Thomas Jefferson, James Madison, James Monroe, and, of course, the father of our country and its first president, George Washington.

It might be assumed that a state that makes so much fuss about its illustrious history would tend to be stuffy and old fashioned. Not so. For, even though we Virginians are proud as can be of our significant past, we're definitely not stuck in it. While reverently protecting and preserving our historical treasures, we are simultaneously moving confidently into the twenty-first century, embracing the new technologies and expanding cultural opportunities that come with it.

Virginia is also a veritable study in contrasts—a conflicting, yet pleasing blend of old and new, rural and cosmopolitan, traditional and high tech, modest and outlandish. We play host to renowned symphony orchestras and old-time fiddlers. We offer classical ballets and flatfooting jamborees; polo matches and mule-jumping competitions. We honor civil war heroes and civil rights leaders. And the same state that once housed the Capital of the Confederacy was also the first state in the nation to elect an African American governor, L. Douglas Wilder, the grandson of former slaves.

Along with contrast, diversity abounds here. In a state that is divided into three distinct and different physical regions, we happily enjoy a diverse mixture of landscapes and topography that yield a feast for the eyes and provide abundant opportunities for outdoor pursuits. From the lofty peaks of the Appalachian Mountains in the west, across the vast and gentle Piedmont, and on to the eastern coastal plain, Virginia has it all. Its mighty rivers and pure mountain streams, glistening lakes, lush forests, and clean, sandy beaches provide endless recreational activities from fishing, swimming, and boating to hiking, rock climbing, and snowboarding.

Virginia's more than seven million citizens are as diverse as its terrain. We're a mixture of nearly every known social, ethnic, and racial group, woven together to create a colorful, vibrant, and interesting tapestry. Ethnic festivals are popular throughout the state, as fun-loving people of all backgrounds come out to share and enjoy each other's foods, music, and crafts. And, although old-time favorites like Virginia ham, fried chicken, and apple pie are still popular at dining establishments across the state, you're also sure to find curry, enchiladas, teriyaki, baklava, and many other ethnic specialties. Variety truly is the spice of life here.

While some areas of Virginia have changed little over the years and still hold on steadfastly to old ways and customs, other regions of the state lead the nation in the fields of technology, science, and medicine. Although we are proud of our rich past, we are equally proud of what we have become and where we are headed.

Fortunately, through all the change and progress, we have managed to retain many of our more endearing "old-fashioned" qualities, such as good manners, friendliness, humor, kindness, and a healthy amount of that famous southern hospitality. Some things, after all, are fine just the way they are.

Opposite page: *From the top of Humpback Rocks, a hiker watches the drama of a Blue Ridge Mountains sunset unfold. Named for their humpback shape, the rock outcrop can be reached via a short trail from the Blue Ridge Parkway. The trail is steep, but the splendid views make the effort worthwhile.*

Chapter One

The Coastal Plain
Sculpted by Water

Virginia's mainland rises westward from the flat and sandy Coastal Plain, or Tidewater. Four mighty rivers divide the upper Tidewater into separate peninsulas, or necks, as they journey from the elevations of the Appalachian Mountains to one of the world's largest estuaries, the Chesapeake Bay. The bay is the heart of Virginia's coast, providing a livelihood for generations of watermen, a playground for boaters and anglers, and a sanctuary for waterfowl and other marine life.

The Northern Neck, sandwiched between the Potomac and Rappahannock rivers, and Middle Neck, stretched between the Rappahannock and York, are both quiet, rural areas. Fishing vessels and pleasure boats ply the myriad creeks and inlets scoured out by the rivers and bay, slipping in and out of busy marinas and quiet fishing villages. Roadside stands offer local fruits and vegetables to passersby, while eateries entice them with promises of fresh bay shellfish.

Between the York and James rivers, on a finger of land known as the Peninsula, the Colonial Triangle of Jamestown, Williamsburg, and Yorktown is a mecca for American history buffs. Remarkably, 174 years of English colonization in the New World began and ended just twenty miles apart on this small piece of American soil. The Peninsula's enormous wealth of preserved and reconstructed historic attractions draws visitors from around the world.

One of Virginia's largest metropolitan areas is Hampton Roads. The name, which originally referred to the large, natural harbor at the mouth of the Chesapeake Bay, is now commonly used to describe all of the surrounding area, including the cities of Hampton, Newport News, Norfolk, Portsmouth, Chesapeake, Suffolk, and Virginia Beach.

Given its strategic position, Hampton Roads quickly developed into a hub of maritime and military activity. Norfolk is home to the world's largest naval base; Portsmouth claims the nation's oldest and largest naval shipyard; Newport News has its immense shipbuilding facility; and Hampton houses NASA's Langley Research Center.

The state's largest city, Virginia Beach, is, first and foremost, a resort town. Its lively beachfront boardwalk is lined with busy hotels, shops, and restaurants, and away from the congested strip, state parks and wildlife refuges offer a more tranquil coastal environment.

Until the Chesapeake Bay Bridge-Tunnel was completed in 1964, residents of Virginia's Eastern Shore were isolated from the rest of the state, relying on ferries to travel to its mainland. Today, the bridge connects the narrow southern tip of the Delmarva Peninsula to Virginia Beach, 17.6 miles and another world away.

A brilliant sunset paints the skies over the Chesapeake Bay, near Kiptopeke State Park, at the southern end of Virginia's share of the Delmarva Peninsula.

Opposite page: The Colonial Williamsburg Fifes and Drums march in front of the Governor's Palace. Passing by picture-snapping spectators and flag-waving children, their processional takes them down Duke of Gloucester Street to the Capitol Building.

Right: *Adjacent to the original settlement site, known as Historic Jamestowne, the Jamestown Settlement is a living history center that portrays the people who settled Jamestown in the seventeenth-century and the natives who witnessed their arrival. It includes a re-created fort and a Powhatan village, as well as replicas of the three ships.*

At Jamestown Settlement, a historical interpreter demonstrates seventeenth-century food preparation inside the re-created colonists' fort.

Life slows down on the Eastern Shore. Pancake-flat farm fields stretch along its one main highway. Side roads journey east to the Atlantic or west to the Chesapeake Bay, passing through tiny, weathered towns, some dating to the 1600s. Like their ancestors before them, most of the hard-working residents make their living from agriculture or on the water.

The peninsula's largest town is Chincoteague, famous for its oysters and a small horse named Misty. One of a herd of horses that has roamed wild for centuries on Assateague Island, Misty became the subject of Marguerite Henry's beloved book, *Misty of Chincoteague*. The origin of these captivating ponies remains uncertain, helping to create an aura of mystery around this enchanting island.

*Statues of Pocahontas and Captain John Smith are found at Historic Jamestowne,
the site of the first settlement, on Jamestown Island.*

Colonial Williamsburg, Virginia's second capital, is now the nation's largest living history museum, with more than five hundred restored or reconstructed buildings occupying more than three hundred acres. The majority of these structures are located along Duke of Gloucester Street.

Left: *Costumed interpreters at Colonial Williamsburg ceremoniously lower the British flag at the Capitol Building, re-creating the scene that followed the colonists' hearing news of the signing of the Declaration of Independence in 1776.*

Above: *As the Colonial Williamsburg Fifes and Drums make their way down Duke of Gloucester Street, a friendly drum major gestures to the crowd of spectators.*

Tiny Yorktown was the scene of a fierce siege by American troops in the fall of 1781. General Cornwallis supposedly made his headquarters in a cave on the town's waterfront during Washington's bombardment of the British army. Today, Yorktown's streets are lined with dozens of seventeenth- and eighteenth-century homes and buildings.

Opposite page: Sheep graze contentedly near the replica of William Robertson's windmill in Colonial Williamsburg. Colonists relied on mills of this type to supply them with ground grains for bread making.

Above: *On October 19, 1781, British General Cornwallis surrendered his troops to General Washington at Yorktown, marking the end of the Revolution. The Articles of Capitulation were worked out at the farmhouse of Augustine Moore. The Moore House is now part of the Colonial National Historical Park.*

Left: *British soldiers fire a cannon during a Revolutionary War re-enactment at Yorktown Battlefield, one of a full slate of events held throughout the year by the National Park Service.*

Yorktown Battlefield was the site of the last battle of the Revolutionary War, where 174 years of English colonization in America came to a close. While Cornwallis's defeated troops marched across "Surrender Field," between the lines of the Continental Army and the French allies, a band played "The World Turned Upside Down."

Lights from Yorktown's George P. Coleman Bridge reflect in the York River, as the first rays of sunrise turn the water a soft pink. The bridge connects York County to the County of Gloucester on Virginia's Middle Neck.

Above: *Many grand colonial plantations occupy the banks of the James River, between Richmond and Williamsburg. Established in 1613, the Shirley Plantation—owned, farmed, and occupied by the same family for eleven generations—is Virginia's oldest. The mansion and outbuildings offer visitors a fascinating look at plantation life.*

Right: *Purportedly designed by noted English architect Sir Christopher Wren, the Wren Building, at Williamsburg's College of William and Mary, is the oldest academic building in continuous use in the nation. Thomas Jefferson, James Monroe, and John Tyler are among the famous alumni of the second oldest university in the country.*

Left: *Since 1958, oyster fans have filled the tiny Middle Neck town of Urbanna for its annual Oyster Festival. The highlight is the Oyster Shucking Contest, when eager shuckers compete for the state championship title and the chance to progress to the National Oyster Shucking Championship in Maryland.*

Below: *George Washington Birthplace National Monument, on the Northern Neck, preserves the site of the Washington plantation, where our first president was born in 1732. The home was destroyed by fire in 1779, but a memorial house and dependencies were constructed in 1931. Generations of Washingtons rest here in the family burial grounds.*

Visitors to the Westmoreland Berry Farm, on the Northern Neck, might be surprised to see goats peering down at them from the ingenious goat walk. The sure-footed acrobats clamber across a ramp, twenty feet off the ground, enticed by the goat chow enchanted visitors offer up to them via a pulley system.

A statue of Mr. Peanut—Planters Peanuts' dapper, monocled mascot—stands proudly in his hometown of Suffolk. Planters moved its operation to Suffolk in 1913, and in 1916, Mr. Peanut emerged as the company's trademark.

With construction beginning in 1632, Historic St. Luke's Church in Smithfield is the nation's oldest existing church of English foundation, as well as the only surviving original Gothic structure in the country. Inside is a 1630 English chamber organ, said to be the oldest intact organ in America.

Above: *The Great Dismal Swamp National Wildlife Refuge encompasses more than 111,000 acres in southeastern Virginia and northeastern North Carolina. Shrouded in mystery and rich in lore, the cypress swamps, forested wetlands, marshes, and bogs, along with a 3,100-acre natural lake, support a huge variety of flora and fauna.*

Right: *The shady, tree-lined streets of Portsmouth's Olde Towne Historic District pass by an impressive collection of elegant, centuries-old homes, with gas lights and flower plantings adding to the charm. The port town, on the Elizabeth River, holds three centuries of history.*

St. Paul's Church (c.1739) in downtown Norfolk was the only building in the city that survived the bombardment of British Lord Dunsmore on New Year's Day 1776. The church didn't make it through completely unharmed, however, as evidenced by the British cannonball still lodged in its south wall.

During a Revolutionary War–era re-enactment at Endview Plantation in Newport News, a young costumed re-enactor demonstrates a hoop toy from the eighteenth century.

Opposite page: Beautiful azaleas grace the front of the Douglas MacArthur Memorial in downtown Norfolk. The building contains the remains of the renowned general and his wife, a Norfolk native, as well as exhibits tracing his impressive military career.

Viewed from Portsmouth, across the Elizabeth River, Norfolk's downtown skyline and Waterside complex are illuminated for the holidays, part of Virginia's "100 Miles of Lights" celebration.

Above: *Nauticus, Norfolk's impressive National Maritime Center, is a high-tech, hands-on science museum with exhibits on everything from ship design to the weather. Berthed alongside it, in the Elizabeth River, is the decommissioned* Wisconsin, *one of the largest battleships ever built by the U.S. Navy.*

Right: *In her role as Ship's Sponsor, First Lady Laura Bush christens the Virginia-class submarine* Texas, *named for her native state, at a ceremony at Northrop Grumman Newport News. With 19,000 employees, the enormous ship building facility is the Old Dominion's largest industrial employer.*

Opposite page: *The topsail passenger schooner,* American Rover, *sails from Norfolk's Waterside, offering narrated tours of Hampton Roads' historical harbor.*

An F/A-18 jet hits Mach 1 during an air show at the Oceana Naval Air Station. The show is one of the many events that take place during the Neptune Festival, Virginia Beach's biggest bash of the year.

Opposite page: *Beneath the pink sky of dusk, the lights at a busy Chesapeake shipyard cast reflections in the Elizabeth River.*

Things are quiet at sunrise in this amusement park on the Virginia Beach boardwalk, but soon these prancing horses will once again be carrying giggling children on a magical fantasy ride.

Left: *On a beautiful day at Virginia Beach's annual Neptune Festival, a dad introduces his gleeful toddler to the joys of playing in the surf.*

Below: *A contestant "shoots the curl" at a surfing competition during Boardwalk Weekend, the culmination of the two-week Neptune Festival, ranked among the top ten festivals in the Southeast.*

Above: *A friendly Uncle Sam makes an appearance at an air show at the Oceana Naval Air Station during the Neptune Festival.*

Left: *The Cape Henry Memorial stands in the middle of the Fort Story Army Base in Virginia Beach. It was here, on April 26, 1607, that the Jamestown settlers first landed in the New World. The memorial replaced the original wooden cross erected by the settlers in gratitude for their safe crossing.*

*Located a short drive south of the bustle of the Virginia Beach "strip," Back Bay
National Wildlife Refuge offers a more serene coastal experience. With more than
8,000 acres of varied habitat, this thin strip of coast is a haven for migrating birds
and year-round wildlife.*

Knarred and twisted tree trunks protrude from the dark, brooding waters of a bald cypress swamp at First Landing State Park. This most visited of Virginia's state parks lies at the mouth of the Chesapeake Bay, just north of Virginia Beach's resort area.

Since 1857, the light from the candy-striped Assateague Island lighthouse has warned mariners of the area's dangerous shoals. The beacon is located within the Chincoteague National Wildlife Refuge.

Snow geese lift off from a pond in Chincoteague National Wildlife Refuge on Assateague Island. The refuge's prime habitat and its location along the Atlantic Flyway make it an important stopover for migratory birds and waterfowl, as well as a permanent home for many other bird and animal species.

The wildlife of Chincoteague National Wildlife Refuge is easily observed from your car or from viewing platforms accessed by easy trails. These snowy egrets busily fish for breakfast in a ditch beside the road.

A wild Chincoteague pony grazes on dune grass as the sun sets on Assateague Island. The most romantic explanation of the small horses' origin is that their ancestors swam ashore from a wrecked Spanish galleon. More likely, they descend from domesticated stock of early settlers who grazed their horses on the island to avoid mainland taxes.

At the wildly popular annual Pony Swim and Auction, "saltwater cowboys" round up the refuge's ponies, swim them across Chincoteague Bay, and sell off many of the young at the next day's auction in town. A throng of enthusiastic fans cheers on the horses during their swim.

Above: *Tangier Island sits in the middle of the Chesapeake Bay, approximately fourteen miles offshore from the Northern Neck. Residents of the tiny island make their living from the bay and the visitors who come on tour boats during the warm months.*

Left: *After unloading his catch, a fisherman at Chincoteague's harbor straightens his nets and readies his vessel for the next trip.*

An old boat, its fishing days long since passed, lies abandoned in the weeds along an inlet in the tiny coastal town of Oyster. Like most Eastern Shore communities, life in Oyster revolves around the water.

Chapter Two

The Piedmont
Heartland of the Commonwealth

Virginia's sprawling mid-section, or Piedmont, begins in the eastern foothills of the Blue Ridge Mountains and stretches to the Fall Line, that linear zone where the hard metamorphic rock of the central plain gives way to the soft, sandy soil of the Coastal Plain. This line roughly parallels I-95 as it traverses the state from Alexandria southward through Richmond.

The area surrounding Charlottesville, in the western Piedmont, is known as Jefferson Country, and the eminent statesman's influence is omnipresent in these parts. Thomas Jefferson's architectural and landscaping achievements at his beloved home, Monticello, and the "academical village" of the University of Virginia stand as superb examples of his multifaceted genius. The homes of two of Jefferson's friends and fellow presidents, James Madison and James Monroe, are also nearby.

In the southern Piedmont, farmers tend expansive fields of cotton, corn, tobacco, and those world-famous Virginia peanuts. Small towns and rural areas comprise the bulk of the region, with the larger cities of Lynchburg, Danville, and Martinsville providing a manufacturing base. Anglers and boaters flock here to enjoy two of the state's most popular recreational lakes, Smith Mountain and Buggs Island, while NASCAR fans take in the thrills at Martinsville Speedway.

The northern Piedmont is referred to simply as northern Virginia, but there's nothing simple about it. Sitting on the doorstep of the nation's capital, this immense metropolitan area pulsates with activity. In addition to the federal government spillover, northern Virginia is also home to a vibrant high-tech community.

Abundant career opportunities have brought a population explosion to the area and, along with it, cultural, shopping, and dining venues rivaling any on the East Coast. Of course, historical attractions are plentiful, with Old Town Alexandria, Washington's Mount Vernon, and Arlington National Cemetery heading the must-see list.

Just on the outskirts of all this commotion, another world exists in the tranquil countryside known as Hunt Country. Along its winding country roads, grand estates (belonging to families of Firestones, Mellons, and the like) peek out from behind old, ivy-covered stone walls. Pampered thoroughbreds graze in white-fenced pastures, and life revolves around equestrian events like steeplechases, polo matches, and the age-old aristocratic sport of fox hunting.

Richmond's downtown skyline is viewed through the glass wall of the Virginia War Memorial. More than 11,500 names of Virginians who died in service to their country are engraved on the walls of the memorial's Shrine of Memory.

Opposite page: *In Virginia's western Piedmont, picturesque farms, like this one west of Charlottesville, lie nestled in the foothills of the Blue Ridge Mountains.*

The lights of Washington, D.C.'s monuments are seen in the distance, as dusk descends over the Marine Corps Memorial in Arlington. While the statue depicts the famous flag-raising at Iwo Jima, it is actually a memorial to all marines who have died in the line of duty since 1775.

Virginia's capital since 1779, Richmond is the heart of the Commonwealth. The city has worn many hats over the years. Besides being the hub of state politics, Richmond is also a hub of commercial activity, stemming from its early days of trade on the James River. Currently, it's home to numerous large corporations, as well as a base for education, medical science, and finance.

As the Capital of the Confederacy, Richmond, as well as nearby Petersburg and Fredericksburg, saw intense action during the Civil War. Today, their well-preserved battlefields and excellent museums help visitors to understand the complexity of the events that unfolded in this war-torn region.

Thirty years ago, downtown Richmond was like an aging Southern Belle—still charming, but in need of a face-lift. Thanks to exciting revitalization, her faded beauty is being restored. Once-shabby, boarded-up warehouse districts and riverfront areas are now refurbished and bustling with trendy shops, restaurants, and urban dwellers.

Sunrise at Arlington National Cemetery finds a lone soldier standing guard at the Tomb of the Unknowns. Containing the remains of unknown soldiers from World Wars I and II and the Korean War, the tomb is guarded twenty-four hours a day by members of the Third United States Infantry.

Historic Christ Church, completed in 1773, was the first Episcopal church in Alexandria. Two of its early regular worshippers were George Washington and Robert E. Lee. The Washington family box pew has been preserved in the church.

Right: *From the piazza of his beloved Mount Vernon estate, George Washington enjoyed a panoramic view of the Potomac River. The president made his home at Mount Vernon for more than forty-five years, until his death in 1799.*

Opposite page: *With the sun rising over the nation's capital, the Eternal Flame, which marks the gravesite of John F. Kennedy at Arlington National Cemetery, maintains its steady flicker.*

Mary Ball Washington, mother of George, lived the last seventeen years of her life in this house in Fredericksburg. This home was bought for her by her son.

A fully operational reconstruction of George Washington's Gristmill is located three miles from the main Mount Vernon estate, on the site of the original mill, built in 1770. In addition to being used by the estate, the flours and cornmeal milled here were also sold along the East Coast and abroad.

Opposite page: *An assortment of eighteenth-century medicinal items lines the shelves and counters of the Hugh Mercer Apothecary Shop in Fredericksburg. Dr. Mercer practiced here for fifteen years, serving such patients as George Washington with treatments like snakeroot, crab claws, and leeches.*

Above: *Costumed interpreters work in the kitchen garden at the Claude Moore Colonial Farm in Fairfax County. The farm is a living history site that demonstrates the life of a poor, pre-Revolutionary War family who scratched out a living on a small tenant homestead in northern Virginia.*

Left: *Tucked into the eastern foothills of the Blue Ridge Mountains, quaint little Sperryville is known for its eclectic collection of shops, galleries, eateries, artisans, and antique markets.*

Opposite page: *The entire achingly charming village of Waterford and its surrounding Loudoun County farmland has been designated a National Historic Landmark District, one of only three such landmarks in the nation. Founded by Quakers in 1733, the village holds an impressive collection of restored eighteenth- and nineteenth-century homes and buildings.*

Above: *During the Blackberry Harvest Festival at Hill Top Berry Farm and Winery in Nelson County, eager berry lovers canvass the pick-your-own vines for the most perfect selections of the luscious fruit.*

Right: *Northern Virginia's Sky Meadows State Park is a perfect place to picnic, hunt wildflowers, or hike one of the many trails traversing open pastures or shady woodlands. This family pauses on their hike to admire the view of the surrounding Fauquier County farmland.*

Opposite page: *In the fall, a roadside market near Sperryville entices passersby with displays of seasonal favorites, such as juicy apples fresh from the trees.*

As the Potomac River nears Washington, D.C., in its eastward journey, it builds up
speed and force as it rushes through narrow Mather Gorge, tumbling over a series
of jagged rocks. At Great Falls Park, short trails lead to overlooks that provide prime
viewing opportunities of this dramatic waterway.

In a rural area of Madison County, a field of soybeans glows golden in the warm, late-afternoon light of autumn.

Cowboys and guest participants move two bulls from one pasture to another during a cattle drive at the Marriott Ranch, a 4,200-acre working cattle ranch in Fauquier County. To the surprise of unsuspecting motorists, traffic is occasionally stopped while small herds are driven down a short stretch of road.

Above: *Members of Virginia's Orange County Hunt, led by the hunt master, begin a morning foxhunt on a Fauquier County farm. This age-old sport, brought to America by early English settlers, has deep roots here, and Virginia has more recognized foxhunting clubs than any other state.*

Left: *A group of horse-racing fans enjoys a gourmet picnic at the Middleburg Spring Races. The prestigious annual event, established in 1921, is the oldest sanctioned steeplechase in Virginia.*

Above: *Horses clear an obstacle on the steeplechase course at the Foxfield Races near Charlottesville. This popular central Virginia tradition is held twice a year.*

Left: *Since the 1950s, Charlottesville has celebrated the arrival of spring with its Dogwood Festival, held in April, during the peak of the dogwood season. The Grand Parade, always a highlight of the two-week festival, takes place in the city's downtown.*

Above: *Just outside of Charlottesville, Thomas Jefferson resided at his beloved Monticello, Italian for "little mountain." Over the course of more than forty years, he designed, redesigned, and expanded the home. "Architecture is my delight," he said, "and putting up and pulling down one of my favorite amusements."*

Right: *In addition to his passion for architecture, Jefferson loved mechanical devices and innovations. His study at Monticello featured a revolving bookstand alongside a worktable with a revolving tabletop. The table held a letter-copying device, called a polygraph, which had two pens that moved simultaneously. As he wrote a letter with one pen, the other made a duplicate copy.*

Opposite page: *Thomas Jefferson founded the University of Virginia in Charlottesville in 1819. He also designed its buildings and grounds, which then included the present-day "Lawn" with its magnificent Rotunda, seen here, and surrounding buildings. Now designated a World Heritage Site, Jefferson's "academical village" was one of his proudest achievements.*

Oak Ridge, a grand two-hundred-year-old estate in Nelson County, hosts various special events throughout the year. During a Civil War Encampment re-enactment, two women approach the mansion in period costume.

Above: *Flat-bottomed boats, called batteaux, plied the James River during the late 1700s, transporting goods to Richmond. Costumed crews celebrate that history during the annual Batteau Festival by floating their batteaux down the James on an eight-day voyage from Lynchburg to Richmond, camping at nights in river towns along the route.*

Right: *In 1611, four years after the founding of Jamestown, a second English settlement was established, south of present-day Richmond on the banks of the James River. The Citie of Henricus is being re-created at Henricus Historical Park, where costumed interpreters demonstrate the daily lives of the hardy settlers who inhabited this seventeenth-century wilderness outpost.*

Above: *Patrick Henry lived with his family at Scotchtown Plantation near Ashland from 1771 until 1778. In 1776, Henry became Virginia's first governor and went on to serve three terms.*

Left: *In March 1775, 120 delegates met at Richmond's St. John's Church for the Second Virginia Convention to discuss the impending revolution. It was here, on March 23, that Patrick Henry gave his famous "Give me liberty or give me death" speech.*

Above: *Hanover Tavern is part of the Hanover Courthouse Historic District. Though the earliest section of the present structure dates to 1791, a tavern has occupied this site since 1733. Henry lived at the tavern site in 1763 while he argued a case at the courthouse across the road.*

Right: *Patrick Henry, the "voice of American liberty," died in 1799, at the age of sixty-three. He is buried in a family cemetery at Red Hill, his last home and now the site of the Patrick Henry National Memorial. The grounds include a museum, seven historic buildings, and the gravesite.*

State representatives in the House of Delegates conduct business in the House Chamber, located in the East Wing of the State Capitol Building. The Senate Chamber is located on the opposite end of the building in the West Wing. Another noteworthy design of Thomas Jefferson's, the capitol building underwent a major restoration between 2004 and 2006.

Marking the entrance of Richmond's Capitol Square is a large equestrian statue of George Washington, surrounded by six other Virginia Revolutionary patriots, including Thomas Jefferson, Patrick Henry, and George Mason. Across the street, the Old City Hall is a magnificent Victorian Gothic structure, now used as a private office building.

Opposite page: A life-size statue of George Washington, by French sculptor Jean-Antoine Houdon, stands in the Rotunda of the State Capitol Building in Richmond. The artist created the statue, said to be a nearly perfect likeness, from detailed measurements he took from Washington's body and a plaster mask he made from his face.

Above: *From 1806 to 1812, Thomas Jefferson built his octagonal home, Poplar Forest, near Lynchburg, as his country retreat. After suffering many changes under subsequent owners, the home was rescued in 1984 by a nonprofit corporation dedicated to restoring it to its original state. With the exterior completed in 1998, work continues on the interior.*

This life-size statue of Thomas Jefferson, sculpted from Carrara marble by artist Edward V. Valentine, is the centerpiece of the Palm Court inside Richmond's elegant Jefferson Hotel. The statue stands beneath a magnificent Tiffany stained-glass skylight.

Opposite page: *Each fall, thousands flock to Richmond for the State Fair of Virginia. The huge event features agricultural competitions, rodeos, concerts, lots of good food, and midway excitement galore.*

Ferrum College's annual Blue Ridge Folklife Festival celebrates the state's rural traditions and heritage, with unusual events such as mule jumping, coon dog treeing, sheep herding, and the horse pull shown here. Traditional craft demonstrations, storytelling, quilt shows, music, and food are also featured.

Opposite page: *Dinwiddie County peanut farmer, Billy Bain, checks the moisture level of his peanuts during the September harvest. The Old Dominion, famous for its gourmet peanuts, has some three hundred peanut farms that produce more than a hundred million pounds of the tasty little nuts annually.*

Left: *Grapevines heavy with ripened fruit bask in the day's last rays of sunshine at Oakencroft Vineyard and Winery, near Charlottesville. From just six farm wineries in 1979, Virginia's wine industry has flourished in recent years, to more than ninety in 2005, ranking it fifth among the nation's grape-growing states.*

Above: *James River State Park, in Buckingham County, is Virginia's newest state park, offering camping, hiking, boating, and fishing. From the Tye River Overlook, hikers on the Cabell Trail are rewarded with a stunning view of a railroad bridge over the Tye River near its confluence with the James.*

Above: *The home of Wilmer McLean, in the Village of Appomattox Court House (now part of the Appomattox Court House National Historical Park), was used as the meeting site where General Robert E. Lee surrendered his army to Lieutenant General Ulysses S. Grant, effectively ending the Civil War in 1865.*

Right: *Generals Lee and Grant met in the parlor of the McLean House on April 9, 1865, to execute the terms of Lee's surrender. In a cordial meeting that lasted little more than ninety minutes, the war that had divided our nation for four years came to an end.*

*At the Booker T. Washington National Monument in Hardy, a reconstructed
cabin stands on the Burroughs farm, where Washington was born and raised in
slavery. His mother was a cook, and their one-room cabin also served as a kitchen.
Washington became America's foremost black educator and founder of Alabama's
Tuskegee Institute.*

Right: *In Bedford, the Elks National Home, a retirement community for members of the Benevolent and Protective Order of Elks in the United States, draws as many as 100,000 visitors each year to view its dazzling Christmas light display.*

Opposite page: *In 1901, the city of Petersburg restored the abandoned 1735 Old Blandford Church and delegated it to the Ladies Memorial Association for a Memorial Chapel and Confederate Shrine. Fifteen Confederate states placed stained-glass windows, created by Louis Comfort Tiffany, in the memorial. Virginia's window, pictured here, features Saint John beneath the state seal.*

Below: *Dawn at Smith Mountain Lake finds a couple and their dog enjoying a quiet moment on their dock. With over 500 miles of shoreline, this most popular of Virginia's lakes is a mecca for water-sport enthusiasts, both vacationer and full-time residents alike.*

THERE STANDS JACKSON LIKE A STONE WALL

Previous pages: *A statue of General Thomas "Stonewall" Jackson looks toward the sunset at Manassas National Battlefield. It was here, in 1861, during the Battle of First Manassas, the first major battle of the war, that Jackson's steadfast determination won him his famous nickname and the Confederates a hard-fought victory.*

Above: *Salem Church, near Fredericksburg, is part of the Fredericksburg and Spotsylvania Court House National Military Park. The church served as a hospital during the Battle of Chancellorsville, and it became a refugee center during the Battle of Fredericksburg for civilians fleeing that war-ravaged city.*

Twenty hours of the most intense fighting of the Civil War transpired at the "Bloody Angle" during the Battle of Spotsylvania Court House in May 1864. A staggering number of lives were lost during this frenzied, hand-to-hand combat, where the barrage of bullets was so forceful that it toppled a twenty-two-inch oak tree.

At the Petersburg National Battlefield Park, a cannon is brought onto the battlefield by re-enactors during a living history program.

Opposite page: *Located to the west of the Piedmont region, the Battle of New Market is re-enacted annually at the New Market Battlefield State Historical Park. This battle is most notable for the 257 Virginia Military Institute cadets who marched from Lexington to reinforce the southern ranks and help to secure one of the last Confederate victories in the Shenandoah Valley.*

Right: *This young duo got into the act during a re-enactment of the Battle of New Market. This event, unique in that it is staged on the original battlefield, is the oldest annual battle re-enactment in the country.*

Below: *During a Memorial Day illumination ceremony at the National Cemetery in Fredericksburg, a woman kneels at the grave of her great-great uncle, who died at Bloody Angle during the Civil War.*

Chapter Three

The Western Highlands
Appalachian Splendor

The western reaches of Virginia lie within the Appalachians, the ancient mountain chain that extends from Alabama to Canada. Though they once stood as tall as the Alps, millennia of weathering have worn them down to today's more modest size.

The Blue Ridge Mountains are the easternmost range of the Central Appalachians in Virginia. These beautiful, misty blue hills run in a southwesterly direction through western Virginia, reaching ever higher as they approach the North Carolina border. Rising to the west like a blue wall, the Allegheny range ripples through a series of mountain ridges and high valleys along Virginia's border before undulating off into neighboring West Virginia.

Nestled between these two majestic mountain ranges is the Shenandoah Valley. The fertile and bucolic Shenandoah (from an Indian word meaning "Daughter of the Stars") was settled by German, Scotch-Irish, and English farmers in the early 1700s. Dubbed the "Breadbasket of the Confederacy" during the Civil War, when it provided food supplies for the Southern army, the valley still has a strong agricultural presence today. Small cities and towns are interspersed with rural areas where family farms, complete with grazing cows and the smell of freshly mowed hay, still prevail.

The mountains reach their loftiest heights in southwestern Virginia, where, at 5,729 feet, Mount Rogers stands as the highest peak in the state. Nearby, Virginia's portion of the New River, the second oldest river in the world (only the Nile is older) flows through the scenic New River Valley.

Mountain music is prevalent throughout the western highlands. But in southwest Virginia, where bluegrass jamborees, hoedowns, and fiddlers' conventions occur weekly, it's sacred. Bristol, on the Virginia-Tennessee border, is known as the Birthplace of Country Music. In 1927, a talent scout from the Victor Recording Company discovered the now legendary Carter Family—A. P., Sara, and Maybelle—performing beautiful mountain ballads in nearby Maces Spring. He took them to Bristol, where they participated in the famous Bristol recording sessions, called the "Big Bang of Country Music."

Extreme southwestern Virginia is coal country. Since the Pocahontas Coalfield opened in 1882, King Coal has fueled the area's economy. This wild and rugged land is part of the Cumberland Plateau, the principal range of the Southern Appalachians. At the westernmost tip of the state, at its border with Kentucky and Tennessee, Daniel Boone blazed out the Wilderness Road through the Cumberland Gap, a break in the Appalachians through which westward-heading pioneers could pass.

Western Virginia's mountains, rivers, lakes, and streams make it a popular playground. Outdoor-sports enthusiasts flock here to hike, camp, boat, fish, swim, mountain bike, rock climb, and snow ski. Two national parks, Shenandoah and Blue Ridge Parkway, protect the scenic splendor and historic integrity of Virginia's Blue Ridge Mountains. They offer a paradise of quiet, forested hiking trails, cool streams and waterfalls, spectacular flora and fauna, inviting lodges and campgrounds, and interesting historic exhibits, as well as breathtaking views from their famous lofty overlooks.

The Link Farm Covered Bridge near Newport dates from 1912. Now privately owned and maintained, the fifty-foot modified Burr-truss bridge over Sinking Creek is one of eight remaining covered bridges in Virginia.

Opposite page: *A short one-mile trek to Little Stony Man Cliffs in Shenandoah National Park rewards hikers with a grand view. In the distance, the park's Skyline Drive twists and winds along the crest of the Blue Ridge Mountains.*

From the Moorman's River Overlook in Shenandoah National Park, fog lingers in the foothills of the Piedmont, as the rising sun penetrates the clouds.

A hiker treks along the Appalachian Trail through the fog and ferns in Shenandoah National Park. One-fourth of the famous 2,100-mile Maine to Georgia trail lies in Virginia, with a ninety-five-mile segment running the entire length of the park.

Opposite page: Woodland sunflowers line the banks along Skyline Drive on its 105-mile route through Shenandoah National Park. With approximately 862 species of wildflowers represented in the park, there is always something in bloom, from early spring through the fall.

A fawn receives a face washing from its mother at Big Meadows in Shenandoah National Park. Whitetail deer are the most frequently spotted of the park's fifty-plus mammal species. In June, Big Meadows is a popular spot for watching fawns frolicking or nursing.

Above: *A hot August evening brought these kids to the South Fork of the Shenandoah River in Page County. This area, with the Compton Cliffs in the background, is one of the most scenic stretches along the river.*

Left: *At the J. P. Russell Orchard in Frederick County, near Winchester, the spring apple bloom is an awesome sight. Frederick County harvests more than three million bushels of the delicious fruits per year, making it the leading apple-producing county in the state.*

Opposite page: *Fall is in the air at the Virginia Farm Market in Winchester. Shoppers load up on local apple products and choose the perfect Halloween pumpkin.*

Dancers in period dress parade down Staunton's Main Street during the city's annual Victorian festival. Staunton's five historic districts are showcases of beautifully restored nineteenth-century architecture. The Shenandoah Valley's "Queen City" is also the birthplace of our twenty-eighth president, Woodrow Wilson.

Opposite page: *Visitors pause to admire Saracen's Tent, a magnificent drapery formation at Luray Caverns, the largest and most visited caverns in the eastern United States. This United States natural landmark contains a wide assortment of formations, columns, and pools, as well as the world's only Stalacpipe Organ.*

The competition gets heated between participants in a grape-stomping contest at a Harvest Festival at Shenandoah Vineyards in Edinburg. Established in 1976, Shenandoah Vineyards is the valley's oldest winery.

Above: *Hay bales dot a field near Swoope, in western Augusta County. The bucolic countryside here remains agricultural, for now, but it is threatened by the increasing land needs of a growing population.*

Below: *A Mennonite couple sets out in their buggy to visit their daughter in her nearby home. The Shenandoah Valley has a thriving Mennonite population, concentrated largely west of the town of Dayton, in Rockingham County. There, they earn their living mainly through agricultural pursuits.*

Pigtailed Mennonite girls participate in a game of softball during recess at their school in Rockingham County. Proper attire for girls includes pretty, cotton dresses, sewn by their mothers. Shoes are optional.

Opposite page: *Wade's Mill, in Rockbridge County, has been grinding since 1750, powered by its twenty-one-foot water wheel. The milling tradition continues with its current owners, who grind and sell a variety of flours. This view is from one of the beautiful theme gardens of the Buffalo Springs Herb Farm adjacent to the mill.*

Left: *McKinley Methodist Church, seen here after a winter snowfall, is one of the many small country churches that grace the rural areas of the Shenandoah Valley. The social lives of these small communities often revolve around their churches.*

The "Old Chapel" stands near the town of Millwood in Clarke County. Lord Fairfax established Frederick Parish here in 1738 as the first Episcopal parish west of the Blue Ridge. This stone chapel was built in 1790 to replace the previous log structure.

Above: *Cadets march across the drill field in a graduation parade at Virginia Military Institute in Lexington. Established in 1839, VMI became the nation's first state-supported military college, and its alumni include many distinguished military leaders. Thomas "Stonewall" Jackson served on the faculty from 1851 until the beginning of the Civil War.*

Opposite page: *Lexington's Washington and Lee University, founded in 1749 as Augusta Academy, is the country's ninth oldest college. Saved from bankruptcy by a gift of stock from George Washington, its name was changed in 1796 to honor its benefactor and again in 1870 to honor its most famous president, Robert E. Lee. This view is of the Lee Chapel.*

Above: *Robert E. Lee's office, while president of Washington and Lee University, was in the lower level of the Lee Chapel, now the Lee Chapel and Museum. The chapel houses the remains of Lee and his family in a family crypt, as well as this famous sculpture of the Recumbent Lee by Edward Valentine.*

Above: *At a powwow held at the Natural Bridge of Virginia's living history Monacan Nation village, a participant takes part in a ceremonial Blanket Dance. Powwows are held throughout Virginia by the eight state-recognized Indian tribes, many of whom proudly trace their history back to the Great Chief Powhatan.*

Opposite page: *On the wall of the Natural Bridge of Virginia, a mammoth limestone arch 90 feet wide and 215 feet high, a young George Washington carved his initials while surveying in 1750. Thomas Jefferson purchased it in 1774 from King George III, calling it "the most sublime of nature's work."*

Highland County, the most sparsely populated and remote county in Virginia, is said to have more sheep than people. Nestled within the ridges of the Allegheny Mountains, the county is made up of tiny towns and farming communities, like Hightown, pictured here.

Opposite page: A bucket collects the sweet sap from a sugar maple tree at Eagle's Sugar Camp in Highland County. After collection, the sugar is boiled and made into maple products. Visitors can watch the syrup-making process at the county's sugar camps during the annual Maple Festival in March.

Above: *The first of two public bath buildings at the Historic Jefferson Pools in Warm Springs opened in 1761, making it the oldest spa structure in America. The mineral baths were named in honor of Thomas Jefferson, who spent three weeks here in 1818 "taking the waters" for his rheumatism.*

Right: *Kids play in the water of Dunlap Creek at the Humpback Bridge near Covington. Built in 1857 as part of the Kanawha Turnpike, Humpback is Virginia's oldest covered bridge and the only curve-span covered bridge still in existence in the country.*

Opposite page: *At Hightown in Highland County, these professional cowboys have rounded up and corralled a farmer's cattle and are loading them into trailers for transport to a cattle sale.*

Right: *Fog rises over Lake Moomaw on a still October morning. The 2,630-acre lake, straddling Bath and Alleghany counties, was formed by the construction of Gathright Dam, which backs up the Jackson River. The lake's recreation area, part of George Washington National Forest, provides opportunities for fishing, boating, and camping.*

Above: *Near Millboro Springs in Bath County, a fisherwoman enjoys a relaxing morning on the Cow Pasture River fly-fishing for trout. Will there be fish for dinner tonight?*

Pages 116-117: *An autumn storm breaks over Twenty Minute Cliff on the Blue Ridge Parkway. The cliff reportedly got its name from early farmers, who used it to tell time during June and July. When sunlight hit the cliff, they knew they had twenty minutes left to work their fields before sunset.*

Above right : *A winter snow blankets the Humpback Rocks Pioneer Homestead exhibit at Milepost 5.8 on the Blue Ridge Parkway. This collection of buildings, transported here from local farms, includes a log cabin, barn, springhouse, and weasel-proof chicken house, all typical of early Appalachian Mountain farms.*

Right: *Items that would have been used by early mountain settlers fill the tiny cabin at the Humpback Rocks Homestead. They include cooking utensils for the fireplace, a lantern for light, and a mountain dulcimer that would have provided the evening entertainment.*

Opposite page: *Located six miles east of the Blue Ridge Parkway in Nelson County, the spectacular Crabtree Falls are a highlight of the George Washington National Forest. Consisting of a series of five major cascades that drop a total of 1,200 feet, it is one of the highest waterfalls east of the Mississippi.*

Above: *A perfect place to enjoy the beauty of autumn is the Blue Ridge Parkway's Peaks of Otter. A comfortable lakeside lodge is surrounded by the three "peaks"—Harkening Hill, Flat Top, and the majestic Sharp Top, seen here rising above Lake Abbott. All three are accessible via hiking trails.*

Right: *A herd of free-roaming ponies wanders the high country at Grayson Highlands State Park, delighting the hikers who encounter them. This beautiful southwest Virginia park, which sits in the highest lands in the state, offers camping, horseback riding, and hiking, including access to the Appalachian Trail.*

Opposite page: *At Breaks Interstate Park, in the far western reaches of Virginia, at the Kentucky border, fog drifts around the Towers, a rock formation that rises six hundred feet above the Russell Fork River. Over millions of years, the raging water carved out the deepest gorge east of the Mississippi.*

Above: *An early morning kayaker enjoys the peace and tranquility of the lake at Hungry Mother State Park, near Marion. The popular park, which offers a variety of recreational amenities, was one of the six original Civilian Conservation Corps parks that opened in 1936.*

Right: *Burke's Garden, a peaceful little valley tucked high in the Allegheny Mountains in southwest Virginia, got its name in 1748, when a surveyor named James Burke compared it to the Garden of Eden. The remote and fertile valley, also called "God's Thumbprint," is primarily a farming community.*

Opposite page: *In bloom, Rhododendron Gap is a highlight of Mount Rogers National Recreation Area, along the Appalachian Trail in southwest Virginia. The area encompasses approximately 115,000 acres of spruce forests, lush meadows, and rocky balds. It also contains the state's highest mountain, 5,729-foot Mount Rogers.*

Above: *At Mabry Mill, on the Blue Ridge Parkway, visitors of all ages love to join in the flatfooting when bluegrass musicians entertain on Sunday afternoons during the summer.*

Above: *Old-time fiddler Benton Flippen warms up before his competition at the annual Old Fiddler's Convention in Galax. For more than seventy years, hundreds of musicians and thousands of fans have gathered in the small southwest Virginia town each August for this weeklong granddaddy of bluegrass competitions.*

Right: *A hiker participates in a Cake Walk during the Appalachian Trail Days in Damascus. One of the towns through which the famous trail passes, Damascus, known as the "friendliest town on the trail," welcomes thousands of trail enthusiasts to its annual celebration with fun festivities, including the famous Hiker's Parade.*

Right: *Abingdon's Barter Theatre, declared the State Theatre of Virginia, opened in 1933, during the Depression. Hungry, out-of-work actors and playwrights, including Gregory Peck and Tennessee Williams, offered their performances to local, cash-poor farmers, who bartered meat and produce in exchange for tickets—a "ham for Hamlet" concept.*

Below: *The War Memorial Chapel sits on the Blacksburg campus of Virginia Tech, the state's largest university. Built as a tribute to the school's alumni who died in the nation's wars, the inspiring Memorial Court, with its eight massive pylons, sits atop the chapel.*

This Norfolk & Western 611-Class J Steam Locomotive was built in 1950 and retired in 1959. It and other fascinating exhibits make up the Virginia Museum of Transportation, housed in a restored Roanoke railway freight station. They document the history of transportation in the Roanoke Valley, from horse-drawn carriages to airplanes.

The lights come on in Roanoke, as dusk settles in. This lofty panoramic view of western Virginia's largest city and the surrounding hills can be enjoyed from the Mill Mountain Overlook.

Few sights compare with a Blue Ridge sunset, and the Blue Ridge Parkway is a fine spot for viewing the spectacle.